Frequently Asked Questions About
Hummingbirds

ROSE HOUK

WESTERN NATIONAL PARKS ASSOCIATION
Tucson, Arizona

HUMMINGBIRDS *thrive*
in DESERTS, especially CANYONS with streamside vegetation;
in woodlands; and in forests and meadows.

How many species of hummingbirds have been discovered?

Between 330 and 350 species are known, depending upon who's doing the counting. All of them live in the Caribbean and South, Central, and North America. Hummingbirds belong purely to the New World, and they reach greatest numbers and diversity near the Equator. In the United States and Canada, 17 species are known to nest, but another 10 or so have been recorded. These numbers are subject to change, however, as different hummingbirds show up in different places.

Cave Creek in the Chiricahua Mountains hosts hummingbirds.

When and where can I see hummingbirds in the western United States?

The West's subtropical areas offer an exciting variety of species, including rare ones that venture north from Mexico on occasion. One of the best regions is southeast Arizona, particularly canyons in the "sky island" mountain ranges of the Santa Ritas, Santa Catalinas, Chiricahuas, and Huachucas. At The Nature Conservancy's Ramsey Canyon Preserve in the Huachuca Mountains you may see a dozen species beginning in April and peaking during the late summer monsoon rains into mid-September. Big Bend National Park in west Texas claims 15 species of hummers—the highest number recorded in any national park. Other select spots in Texas include Guadalupe National Park, Padre Island, and the Gulf Coast from late summer to early winter; in the western high country in summer; along the Pacific Coast; in the hummingbird aviary at the Arizona-Sonora Desert Museum in Tucson; and at various botanical gardens and preserves throughout the West.

Left: A male broad-billed hummingbird stretches. Below: Big Bend National Park in west Texas has the most species of recorded hummingbirds in the National Park System.

Giant hummingbird: 8½ inches long

What habitats do they prefer?

Hummingbirds thrive in deserts; especially in canyons with streamside vegetation, in woodlands, and in forests and meadows. They live from sea level, into foothills, and up to timberline.

To what scientific order and family do hummingbirds belong?

They are placed, along with the swifts, in the order Apodiformes. The word means "footless," but hummingbirds actually do have small, inconspicuous feet. They use their feet to perch but don't walk on the ground. Hummingbirds belong to the family Trochilidae, which means "small bird."

Bee hummingbird: 2¼ inches long

How big do hummingbirds get? How small?

The giant hummingbird, at about 8½ inches long, is the largest. It resides in South America. The smallest is the bee hummingbird of Cuba, a mere 2¼ inches long. The calliope is the smallest in North America, the largest on this continent is the bluethroated.

Hummingbirds perch on small feet.

How much do they weigh?

Depending on the species, they can weigh between ⅟₁₅ to ¾ of an ounce. On average, though, hummingbirds weigh about ⅟₁₀ of an ounce (3.5 grams), about as much as a single penny. They can increase their weight by half or more as they prepare for migration.

Black-chinned hummingbird

Hummingbirds belong to the family TROCHILIDAE, which means "small bird."

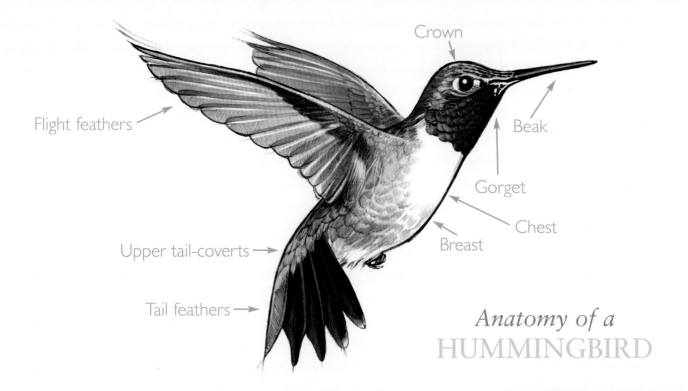

Flight feathers

Crown

Beak

Gorget

Chest

Breast

Upper tail-coverts →

Tail feathers →

Anatomy of a
HUMMINGBIRD

What gives them their iridescent colors?

The gleaming emerald, bronze, and violet colors result from both pigments and, mostly, feather structure. Flat platelets on certain feathers contain bubbles of air that split light into a spectrum of colors, much like a prism. That light then reflects and refracts to our eyes. Thus the iridescent colors change instantaneously depending upon angle of light, the viewer's location, and the birds' constant movements. Rusts, browns, and more subdued colors come from pigmentation alone. Females of some species overall are duller in color than males; in dim light both genders—and juveniles—are dull and thus more difficult to identify.

A buff-bellied hummingbird whose colors arise mostly from special feather structures.

The ruby-throated hummingbird takes its name from the color of the gorget, the bright throat patch. Only males sport the gorget.

What is the bright throat patch called?

It is the gorget, of highly iridescent, specialized feathers. Only males sport the gorget, and not in all species. This eye-catching patch can range from bright red in the male broad-tailed, to scarlet, orange, turquoise, blue, violet, or purple in other species. The ruby-throated hummingbird—the only breeding hummer regularly found east of the Great Plains—takes its name from the color of the gorget. People in the West often think they've seen a ruby-throated, when it's most certainly a broad-tailed.

A hummingbird's *heart* can BEAT more than a THOUSAND times a minute.

Allen's hummingbird has a metabolic rate far greater than that of humans.

How fast is their metabolic rate?

Hummingbirds have an incredibly high metabolism, probably the fastest of any warm-blooded vertebrate in the world except possibly the shrew's. They consume great amounts of oxygen, and their hearts can beat more than a thousand times a minute when they are in pursuit or in display flights. Allen's hummingbird is considered the fastest metabolizing vertebrate known, with a rate 50 times that of humans.

How long do hummingbirds live?

Four to five years on average, although a female broad-tailed in Colorado, banded and tracked in the wild, was known to live to at least 12 years. In captivity, they live longer.

How do hummingbirds stay warm?

By eating and moving almost constantly. Their small body size means a high rate of heat loss, so they must take in a huge number of calories each day just to maintain body temperature.

What do hummingbirds do when it gets cold?

Hummingbirds lack insulating downy feathers that most birds have. Thus, on chilly summer nights at higher elevations, they must do something to survive when the temperature drops. The tiny calliope hummingbird, for example, nests almost to timberline in the Rockies, Sierra Nevada, and other mountain areas.

The solution is an energy-conserving state called torpor. In this slowed-down condition the birds' body temperature, heart rate, and respiration drop significantly. Hummingbirds can remain in torpor for 8 to 12 hours. At dawn they rouse in about 20 minutes to an hour, depending on the bird and how deep into torpor it has gone. If outside temperatures stay cold for longer periods and no food is available, most hummers head south or go downslope.

Most hummingbirds head south or go downslope if outside temperatures stay cold for long periods.

Taking Flight

Most Anna's hummingbirds stay year-round in California, but some go east to Arizona.

How do they fly?

Hummingbirds have an amazing ability to hover for long periods. They also can fly backward, side to side, even briefly upside down. If trapped and trying to escape, they will fly straight up. In hovering flight, they rotate their shoulder joints, turning the wings completely over on the backstroke and forestroke, tracing a figure eight in the air. They achieve lift both in forward and backward motion.

This flight ability derives from a unique wing anatomy—with a long forepart, or "hand," and almost no "arm." The wings, operating much like a helicopter rotor, remain stiff and do not flap or flex as in other birds.

In addition, strong breast muscles power their flight and account for about 30 percent of the birds' weight. Those muscles are suffused with myoglobin and capillaries, thus supplying a greater oxygen supply than in birds that don't have to sustain such vigorous flight.

How fast do hummingbirds beat their wings?

Rapid wingbeats are another hummingbird superlative. The smallest ones exhibit the fastest wingbeats of any bird known—up to 200 beats a second in courtship displays. Larger hummingbirds have fewer wingbeats. On average, however, a North American hummingbird in flight beats its wings about 53 times a second, more than 3,000 times a minute.

BACKWARD FLIGHT   FORWARD FLIGHT

Hummingbirds are FIERCELY *aggressive* against other hummers.

Ruby-throated male (below) and female (above) hummingbirds drink nectar from crimson star columbine.

When is breeding season?

The time of breeding varies with the species—it can be as early as October and November for Anna's, February or March for Costa's. For species such as broad-tailed, rufous, and others, it's spring and summer.

A Costa's hummer feeds on cactus blooms in Arizona.

Do they defend territory?

Hummingbirds are fiercely aggressive against other hummers. They dart at intruders and fan their tail feathers. Males fight competitors and try to impress mates, females protect their young, and both males and females defend nectar sources and feeding territories. If a feeding territory is too large to defend, some birds use another strategy, narrowing down to a fixed daily route called a "trapline." Defensive actions entail costs and benefits—the rewards must be greater than the high cost in energy for the bird.

How do hummingbirds mate?

After a male has adequately advertised himself with the shuttle flight and other courtship displays, with the female's acquiescence copulation takes place. It is a fleeting act, measured in seconds, and happens while the birds are perched or in flight. Mating can be so aggressive it appears the birds are fighting. As soon as the union is consummated, the male is gone.

Nests may also include buds, bark, and bits of DRIED FLOWERS.

Ruby-throated nest with eggs

What are nests made of?

With her bill, the female weaves tiny upright cups—about 2 inches wide—of spider silk, downy plant parts, lichen, and moss. The spider webs hold the nest together and are elastic so the nest can expand to accommodate growing chicks. The soft cottony material lines the nest, and lichen and moss lend camouflage. Nests may also include buds, bark, and bits of dried flowers, and some are constructed to mimic pine cones, mistletoe, or clumps of flood-deposited material. At the hummingbird aviary at the Arizona-Sonora Desert Museum in Tucson, keepers supply hair, fur, sweater yarn, and even dryer lint for hummer nesting material.

Black-chinned hummingbird nesting

Anna's hummingbird nest with young

Broad-billed hummingbird feeding young

Where do hummingbirds usually locate their nests?

Nests are built on branches and twigs of trees and shrubs, occasionally in cactus, in caves or rock crevices, even behind waterfalls. They can be a few inches to many feet off the ground and sometimes are shaded or sheltered by an overhanging branch. The female almost always begins building her nest before mating, taking days to weeks to complete it. Some will return to the same site year after year, building on top of an old nest to create a multistory home, or locating a new nest in place of the old one.

How many eggs does a hummingbird lay?

The female produces two white eggs, two days apart. They are about the size of a pea or bean. She incubates the eggs for 12 to 22 days, a most vulnerable time when accidents, weather, or predators can take a toll. Mortality is high among nestlings too—fewer than half the chicks hatched in a season may live to fledge. If the eggs or young are lost, the female may build another nest, lay a second clutch of eggs, and rear another brood in the same season.

Who rears the young?

A male hummingbird mates with several females in one season and isn't involved in nesting or feeding the young. Parenting is the female's job. She builds and defends the nest and feeds and teaches the young. To feed, she brings in partially digested insects and spiders, stored in her crop and stuffed down into the crops of her offspring. The female also sits on her brood to protect them and keep them warm until they begin to grow their own feathers. If it's hot outside, she shades them with her body and wings.

A calliope
hummingbird
gets fueled at
feeder.

Hummingbirds get protein from spiders
and small insects.

How long before hummingbird young leave the nest?

Nestlings normally begin to fledge (leave the nest) three to four weeks after they're born. Fledging takes time and practice—the young must develop flight feathers and flight muscles. First, the nestlings sit on the edge of the nest, trying out their wings. Then they take off for real, each day venturing a little farther, learning to hover at flowers but staying within "peeping" distance of mom. After both the young have fully fledged, they're usually weaned and on their own within a week. Then they obtain their own food, defend their own territories, find mates, and migrate alone.

What do hummingbirds eat?

Flower nectar, insects, some pollen, at times even tree sap, from holes drilled into trees by other birds. It is the sugar-rich nectar that fuels a hummingbird's all-consuming metabolism and ability to fly. The four-parts-water to one-part-sugar recipe for home bird feeders closely replicates the proportions found in nature. But hummingbirds are carnivores too. They must have protein in the form of spiders and small insects such as aphids, flies, and gnats that they can capture and swallow in flight.

Ruby-throated young in nest

How do they find food?

Hummingbirds find food mostly by sight (they have a poor sense of smell). The birds go from flower to flower, allowing adequate time for each bloom to replenish nectar supplies. Apparently hummingbirds have good spatial memories and can relocate a patch of productive flowers.

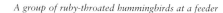

A group of ruby-throated hummingbirds at a feeder

Black-chinned hummingbird
feeds at ocotillo flowers.

What plants do hummingbirds visit for nectar?

At least 150 species of flowering plants in North America have evolved for hummingbird foraging and pollinating. In the West, flowers of agave, ocotillo, cacti, coral bean, penstemon, paintbrush, gilia, salvia, and columbine are among their favorites.

Flower attributes have adapted with hummingbirds in ways that not only benefit but also guarantee the survival of both. Hummers seek out trumpet-shaped flowers, often hanging pendants from stems, frequently red in color, and with large amounts of nectar but little scent. Reservoirs of nectar reside deep in the flower tube, inaccessible to bees and other insects but available to a hummingbird's long bill like a lock to a key.

Barrel cactus blooms

In some tropical species, length and shape of a bird's bill are even more closely matched to flower structure.

In exchange for nectar, hummingbirds perform important pollination services for plants. Anna's hummingbird does this for currant, gooseberry, and monkeyflower, among many others, while the rufous pollinates morning glories and tree tobacco along "nectar corridors" through Mexico and into the Southwest U.S.

How do they eat?

They hover in front of a flower, not landing but dipping their bills into the blossom. It is not the bill but the longer brush-tipped tongue that actually laps in the nectar, using tongue grooves and capillaries to hold it on. When the bird is not eating, its tongue is curled up and laid back over the skull.

How much do they eat?

Hummingbirds must consume about half their body weight each day to support their extreme metabolism. While foraging, they stop frequently for nectar and take small amounts at a time. A single bird may visit a thousand flowers to obtain the 8 to 10 calories it needs in a day. Before a bird settles in for the night, it fills up on as much food as possible, storing it in the crop to be digested during sleep.

Female ruby-throated hummers feed on columbine flowers.

Hummingbirds

How do hummingbirds pollinate plants?

When a hummer dips into a flower, pollen often collects on its head, throat, bill, and stomach. On a visit to another flower of the same species, the bird inadvertently deposits that pollen onto the female part of the flower, providing material for possible fertilization of the plant. Because hummers fly long distances, their pollination services also foster gene exchange between plants.

Magnificent hummingbird

Columbine-red flowers are most attractive to hummingbirds.

Do hummingbirds go only to red flowers?

They do feed from red flowers more often, but they visit pink, purple, yellow, orange, and white ones too. What the birds are really after is sweet and abundant nectar. They will return to that resource, no matter the color of the flower that offers it. Red may have advantages, however. It stands out against a background and is a heat-absorbing color, hence the nectar is warmed and is more available to the birds. Also bees don't see red, largely eliminating them as competitors for nectar.

Broad-billed hummingbird with pollen on bill

Blue-throated hummingbird on an agave plant

must consume about half their body weight each day to support their EXTREME METABOLISM.

Do hummingbirds need water?

Yes, both for drinking and bathing. They take to water in shallow ponds and birdbaths, mist from garden hoses, the spray of waterfalls, even drops on the surface of a leaf. They get plenty of water from nectar too. Hummingbirds are among only a few birds that excrete liquid urine.

Black-chinned hummingbird

Do hummers make sounds?

Some do communicate through calls and songs—consisting mostly of weak chips, squeaks, or chatters—but nothing like the melodies produced by songbirds. What they lack in vocal ability, hummingbirds make up for in buzzing, trilling, and humming sounds arising from movement of their feathers and wings.

What other animal is sometimes mistaken for a hummingbird?

Insects—especially hawkmoths—exhibit much the same behavior and share the same nectar sources. Also called sphinx or hummingbird moths, the hawkmoth hovers in front of flowers as hummingbirds do. But in other ways they are different. The moths are drawn to pale flowers such as datura and evening primrose that are sweetly scented. Hummingbirds lack a well developed sense of smell, so it is not scent but color and nectar abundance that attracts them. Moths feed mostly at night, but at dawn they have been seen competing with hummingbirds for the same nectar.

Costa's hummingbird preening

Hummingbird moth nectaring on bee balm

Insects—especially hawkmoths—exhibit similar behavior and SHARE the same nectar sources.

What preys on hummingbirds?

Larger birds such as crows, jays, and roadrunners are the main predators. Snakes and housecats will also take hummingbirds. Even large insects such as praying mantids can eat a young hummingbird.

What have people called hummingbirds, and what stories do they tell of them?

The Aztec, Maya, Mohave, Pima, Navajo, and Pueblo people have stories about hummingbirds, often ascribing to them an all-powerful role of bringing life and rain. Pueblo pottery is painted with hummingbird designs, and the Hopi in Arizona have a hummingbird katsina (*Tocha*). To the Pima they are "rain birds," and the Mohave say that Hummingbird led them up to this world where they live now. The Navajo equate a many-colored corn with hummingbird, and they call the bird *Da-hi-tu-hi*, "one who brings life." Many other native people have names in their languages for hummingbirds, often describing how they look, act, or sound, or their role in a story.

European explorers to the New World first saw hummingbirds in the Caribbean. Christopher Columbus wrote of a little bird "so different from ours it is a marvel." Hummingbird skins were taken back to European royalty, artists drew them, and naturalists in Italy, Spain, and France described them.

Caribbean Indians called them *colibri*, or at least that was the Spanish rendition of the word that remains in use today. Spanish speakers also called it *pajaro mosca*, "bird fly;" in French it was *le petit mouchet*, "very little fly," and *oiseau-mouche*. By the mid seventeenth century, the English *hum bird*, later *hummingbird*, appeared in writings. To science, each hummingbird has a generic and specific name in Latin.

In the western United States, Meriwether Lewis of the Lewis and Clark Expedition of 1804 to 1806, noted a hummingbird on a nest about to lay eggs. It was a broad-tailed, a common western breeding species, the region's first hummingbird recorded by whites.

Top: Mexican jay
Center: Greater roadrunner
Snakes prey on hummingbirds.

MIGRATORY BIRD *treaties and laws*
protect hummingbirds from EXPLOITATION.

Female ruby-throated hummingbird feeding on cigar plant

What myths have surrounded hummingbirds?

One early belief held that they were half fly and half bird. Another was that they rose from the dead (Franciscan friar Bernardino de Sahagún, in Mexico in the sixteenth century, observed that hummingbirds died in winter but rose from the dead in spring.) People believed hummingbirds fell, rather than flew, backward from flowers; that they survived only on nectar (many died when being shipped from the New World back to the Old because people didn't realize they needed insects for protein); that they sucked nectar from flowers through their bills, like a straw; and that they hitched rides on the backs of geese.

Male Anna's hummingbird dips into a fairy duster flower.

What uses have they been put to?

Early American colonists observed that local Indian chiefs wore hummingbird skins as ear pendants. Euro-Americans shipped hundreds of thousands of skins back to Europe for the feathers, coveted as decoration on hats and dresses or for displays in museums or homes of wealthy patrons. In Mexico, dried powdered hummingbird bodies are still sold to men and women as an attractant to the opposite sex.

Are hummingbirds protected by law?

Yes, migratory bird treaties and laws protect them from exploitation, and the birds cannot be handled or held in captivity without a permit. Banders must be trained and licensed. It is legal, however, for people to put out home feeders filled with sugar water (which should be changed and cleaned often, and not tinted with red food coloring). In the long run it's likely better for hummingbirds to depend more on natural food sources. Thus more people now are attracting hummingbirds by planting gardens of good nectar plants. Native plant nurseries, arboreta, and local Audubon societies can provide information on suitable plants. People can also help by supporting efforts to protect valuable habitat needed for migration corridors.